COMMON

LOVE

LIES

THAT CAN STOP YOU FROM FINDING TRUE LOVE

KINGSLEY OKONKWO

Common Love Lies

Published & Printed in Nigeria by:
Livingproof Press Ltd.
Tel: +234 802 389 1766
E-mail:livingproofpress@yahoo.com

... <u>True</u> Love is invincible facing danger and death... The fire of love stops at nothing - it sweeps everything before it.
Flood waters can't drown love, torrents of rain can't put it out. Love can't be bought, love can't be sold - it's not to be found in the marketplace.

- Song of Solomon 8:6-7[MSG]

CONTENTS

Note to Reader

Love is such a beautiful thing; it's one of the things that makes life worth living. It is one of the best gifts a human can ever give or receive. In fact as the saying goes, the greatest thing you'll ever learn is just to love and be loved in return. It seems everyone hopes to experience it in their lifetime, even if they will only admit it secretly.

But from my years of experience as a relationship coach, I have come to the conclusion that very few people have ever experienced "true love". I actually believe that it seems the more people chase it, the more elusive it becomes. Very few couples describe what they have with their partners as true love and I feel it's because most people have believed the lies told them about love. This has created a need for me to address the COMMON LOVE LIES. I believe that If we can remove the lies, then we can know the truth about love and increase the chances of people actually experiencing true love.
My prayer for you as you read this is that you will come to understand what true love really is and

eliminate all the lies you've believed about love and in doing so that you will experience true love.

With Love,

Kingsley Okonkwo

INTRODUCTION

As I sit at my desk, putting together the different definitions of love I have heard over the years, I can't help but wonder how people arrived at such definitions. To be honest, some of the definitions are direct pointers to why the relationships or marriages never saw the light of day. Which is typical in our time, as a lot of relationships and marriages fail even before they start because of how the parties involved unconsciously define love.

Without mincing words, one of the most misinterpreted, misunderstood and misused words in our world today is the word "LOVE". This might come to you as a surprise since it is used practically everywhere; in songs, adverts, movies, novels, I mean literally everywhere. Interestingly, every one of these platforms paints a different picture when trying to portray love, as such giving people so many exciting yet untrue interpretations of love.

It's sad but a lot of people honestly have no idea what it truly means when they say the three words "I Love You" to someone else. In Fact, most people are actually just in love with the idea of being in love.

What they call love has nothing to do with love. For them everything about love falls within emotional expressions; it's all about the feelings. They are sick when the person they love is not available, they can't breathe when the person is available, they struggle with anxiety when the person is away and they can't think straight when the person is around. They lack self-control and so make poor judgement calls all under the guise of being in love. This is what this generation defines as love. Which makes one ask, *"what is love?"*

This is a very important question because a lot of people make love seem like it is mysterious. Even educated people are completely ignorant when it comes to love. They tell you, "love is a thing of the heart, so follow your heart." Interestingly, in no other field is this mode of operation adopted. Engineers know that there are principles to follow when you need to get a machine moving, medical professionals know that you cannot go with your feelings when prescribing drugs or performing surgeries, and it's the same with love, there are guiding principles for love if you don't want to be hurt.

You see, love is so powerful, a lot of lives have been made better by it. However, a lot more lives have been marred by what they call love. This is because, like I stated earlier, most times what we call love is actually not love. I cannot overemphasize how shocked I am when I hear how people define love. Most times, from their definition, I can tell that what they have is nothing close to love. It might be infatuation; it might even be some sort of obsession or lust but it is definitely not love.

Most times when I teach on love, 2 Samuel 13:1-17 is my go-to scripture and two lines (1 and 15) stand out for me in this long read;

And it came to pass after this, that Absalom the son of David had a fair sister, whose name was Tamar; and Amnon the son of David loved her.

2. And Amnon was so vexed, that he fell sick for his sister Tamar; for she was a virgin; and Amnon thought it hard for him to do anything to her.

3. But Amnon had a friend, whose name was Jonadab, the son of Shimeah David's brother: and Jonadab was a very subtil man.

4. *And he said unto him, Why art thou, being the king's son, lean from day to day? wilt thou not tell me? And Amnon said unto him, I love Tamar, my brother Absalom's sister.*

5. *And Jonadab said unto him, Lay thee down on thy bed, and make thyself sick: and when thy father cometh to see thee, say unto him, I pray thee, let my sister Tamar come, and give me meat, and dress the meat in my sight, that I may see it, and eat it at her hand.*

6. *So Amnon lay down, and made himself sick: and when the king was come to see him, Amnon said unto the king, I pray thee, let Tamar my sister come, and make me a couple of cakes in my sight, that I may eat at her hand.*

7. *Then David sent home to Tamar, saying, Go now to thy brother Amnon's house, and dress him meat.*

8. *So Tamar went to her brother Amnon's house; and he was laid down. And she took flour, and kneaded it, and made cakes in his sight, and did bake the cakes.*

9. *And she took a pan, and poured them out before him; but he refused to eat. And Amnon said, Have out all men from me. And they went out every man from him.*

10. And Amnon said unto Tamar, Bring the meat into the chamber, that I may eat of thine hand. And Tamar took the cakes which she had made, and brought them into the chamber to Amnon her brother.

11. And when she had brought them unto him to eat, he took hold of her, and said unto her, Come lie with me, my sister.

12. And she answered him, Nay, my brother, do not force me; for no such thing ought to be done in Israel: do not thou this folly.

13. And I, whither shall I cause my shame to go? and as for thee, thou shalt be as one of the fools in Israel. Now therefore, I pray thee, speak unto the king; for he will not withhold me from thee.

14. Howbeit he would not hearken unto her voice: but, being stronger than she, forced her, and lay with her.

15. Then Amnon hated her exceedingly; so that the hatred wherewith he hated her was greater than the love wherewith he had loved her. And Amnon said unto her, Arise, be gone.

16. And she said unto him, There is no cause: this evil in sending me away is greater than the other that thou didst unto me. But he would not hearken unto her.

17.   Then he called his servant that ministered unto him, and said, Put now this woman out from me, and bolt the door after her.

However, like I mentioned above, what will determine the success of your relationship or marriage is if the basis for your love is true. The lines above represent the reality of a lot of people in relationships and marriages. In one minute they love someone and then hate them in the next.

I can tell you categorically that a lot of marriages failed before they started because what they were building on was not love, it was mere lies. It's only love that never fails- 1 Corinthians 13:8(KJV). If love is not built on the right foundation, it will take a bitter toll on the individuals involved as we can see from the scripture we read above.

More often than not, the problems people will face in a relationship or marriage will start from misinterpreting the word 'love'. Issues in relationships rise and fall on people's understanding of love. Let me help you uncover some of the most prominent lies which you might have heard and possibly believed but are affecting your experience with finding and sustaining true love.

CHAPTER ONE

COMMON LOVE
LIES

LIE 1

WE WILL FIND OUR
ONE TRUE LOVE

This is the first lie I would like to address. No other love lie has kept as many people single and unhappy for years. The idea of finding your "one true love"- that one mystical and mythical electric and feverish connection with that one person that is totally flawless, understands us the way no other person does, says and does all the perfect things, has exceptional physical features and simply takes your breath away… is unrealistic. No normal human being living on this earth can fit into that description and if by some chance he or she does fit, what is the possibility that they would want you? What if they don't? Your one true love is gone, possibly forever. It's sad, but this belief and expectation in some sort of magical experience is the reason there are so many single or unhappy couples today.

Most people never find that perfect person and even when they seem to, they are bewildered when the feeling doesn't last.

The concept of one true love only happens in movies, not in real life. It's important that I state this here: We *don't find love, we attract love*. So, instead of going in search of one true love and all the fantasies associated with it, your focus should be on attracting wholesome like-minded people who share similar basic but vital values with you and then building love with them.Interestingly, this culture of finding a magical romance is relatively new. It wasn't this common about thirty years ago. It was made popular by movies, cartoons and music. It was then driven by people making a living from the sale of flowers, chocolates, diamond rings, and similar accessories.

In fact, the notion of finding your one true love or soul mate is neither scriptural nor cultural. There is nowhere in scriptures that the Bible says we should marry who we love, it only says we should love who we marry, meaning the commandment to love comes after the choosing or after the marriage and not before.

Husbands, love your wives, just as Christ loved the church and gave himself up for her.
- Ephesians 5:25 [NIV]

The scripture above agrees with how the old cultures also saw love and marriage. People married first and loved after. People never married because of love, they married and then they grew in love with whom they married. Even animals practice the same process, when picking a partner, animals focus on survival, protection, posterity, etc. They don't just pick a mate that they "love", they pick a mate that guarantees survival.

The first marriage in scripture said nothing about love, it was purely functional, God said the man needed a helper, that was it! No emotions consulted, nothing.

I will end this chapter by sharing my parents "love story":

My mom is almost 80 years old and a few months ago I asked her how she met and married my dad. She said she was attending an Anglican youth fellowship and the leader of the fellowship at the time who was a married elder came to her house with my dad who was working in Lagos and looking for a wife.

Prior to their coming, he had asked if there was any good christian girl that the leader knew and the elder said, yes, he knew a good girl who attended his fellowship. So, they both went to visit my mum and made their intentions known. My mum said she looked at my dad and he looked good, he had a job and a friendly disposition so she said yes. In five months, they had their traditional marriage and that was it!

There was nothing like "there's a special man for me". They were introduced, she looked at him, saw that he was healthy, handsome, spoke good English, had the capacity to take care of her and her children when they were born eventually and everything else was fine by her, so she agreed to be his wife. They lived together for over fifty years before my dad passed on. No long story!

I believe this is the reason there were fewer mature singles in those days, unlike now that so many women refuse proposals because their minds are full of Disney level fantasies of a prince charming, so they can't find the average man attractive. Men are also out there looking for supermodels with a touch of prayer warrior.

So, am I saying pick the first person that comes your way or that you should marry someone you don't like? Definitely not! I'm not in any way saying that, I'm simply emphasizing on the fact that most times because we have the notion of a one true love that exists somewhere it clouds our minds from sincerely giving the people around us a chance. If anything they will be friend-zoned simply because we believe there's one special person out there who is our true love.

Don't believe the lie that you have one special person out there that will automatically click with you, instead find a good man or woman and build love together.

LIE 2

LOVE IS A FEELING

"*Love is patient, love is kind, it is not jealous; love does not brag, it is not arrogant. It does not act disgracefully, it does not seek its own benefit; it is not provoked, does not keep an account of a wrong suffered, it does not rejoice in unrighteousness, but rejoices with the truth; it keeps every confidence, it believes all things, hopes all things, endures all things. Love never fails; ..."*

This lie has caused more divorces and heartbreaks than any other love lie. Most people have come to equate love with feelings and you can't blame them. The reason is obvious, the media projects love in such an exciting and attractive way that you literally feel the passion and inseparable bond between the lovers. It's usually such a beautiful feeling that somewhere within your heart you secretly long for that kind of feeling in your relationship but that's not the reality of love. Now, I don't undermine the fact that you might feel a form of attraction to an individual when you love them but it's important you note that your feeling does not make it love.

Love is not a feeling, it is much more than that; it is a sacrifice for another person's good, it is a commitment. Feelings are fickle and won't always be there, love requires more action than affection, it's not a state you are in but a statement of promise to be there for someone through thick and thin. Yes, love has feelings but in itself, it is not a feeling.

Google defines feelings as an emotional state or reaction. From this definition, we can see that a feeling is an emotional state which means that it is a condition that a person is in at a specific time. So, a person can feel they love you now and when they find someone richer or more beautiful, they can also begin to have feelings for them which changes the way they feel about you. Feelings are temporary. They are subject to change. Sadly, a lot of single people go ahead to make bold permanent decisions based on these temporary feelings.

A lot of the intense feelings people have for others at first sight falls between infatuation, obsession and lust. These feelings are brought about by chemicals in the brain, such as dopamine; the feel-good hormone, Oxytocin- the love hormone, Cortisol and Serotonin. An eye opening research was conducted a while ago, the brains of people madly in love were scanned. The result showed a heavy surge of dopamine, a neurotransmitter in the brain's reward system that helps people feel pleasure. Dopamine, along with other chemicals, gives people that energy, focus, and obsession they feel when they are wild about someone. Some of these chemicals are released when someone receives as little as a hug or touch from someone they admire.

Many singles have been thrown off their feet by a simple touch, a pleasant word or a kind gesture. Every single feel-good hormone in their bodies told them it was true love. If you asked them what they loved about him or her, they really couldn't say something worthwhile, they are overwhelmed by what they feel. The truth is, if someone loves you and doesn't know why, when they begin to hate you, they also will not know why. This is because most times our feelings are induced by chemicals in the brain and most people can't tell the difference.

I usually tell people that fake love and true love are identical twins; they have the same symptoms but time is what helps you differentiate them. Recent research showed that the romantic passion people feel will usually expire between two to three years. This does not necessarily mean that the relationship will break up completely, it only shows that the spark or passion they feel will end at about that time. True love, on the other hand, is beyond a chemical reaction or feeling. True love has genuine substance which makes it grow stronger as the years go by. Let's take a look at 2 Samuel 13 (NLT) once again;

Prince Absalom, David's son, had a beautiful sister named Tamar. And Prince Amnon (her half brother) fell desperately in love with her. Amnon became so tormented by his love for her that he became ill. He had no way of talking to her, for the girls and young men were kept strictly apart. But Amnon had a very crafty friend—his cousin Jonadab (the son of David's brother Shimeah).

One day Jonadab said to Amnon, "What's the trouble? Why should the son of a king look so haggard morning after morning?"

So Amnon told him, "I am in love with Tamar, my half sister."

"Well," Jonadab said, "I'll tell you what to do. Go back to bed and pretend you are sick; when your father comes to see you, ask him to let Tamar come and prepare some food for you. Tell him you'll feel better if she feeds you."

So Amnon did. And when the king came to see him,

Amnon asked him for this favor—that his sister Tamar be permitted to come and cook a little something for him to eat. David agreed and sent word to Tamar to go to Amnon's quarters and prepare some food for him. So she did and went into his bedroom so that he could watch her mix some dough; then she baked some special bread for him. But when she set the serving tray before him, he refused to eat!

"Everyone get out of here," he told his servants; so they all left the apartment.

Then he said to Tamar, "Now bring me the food again here in my bedroom and feed it to me." So Tamar took it to him. But as she was standing there before him, he grabbed her and demanded, "Come to bed with me, my darling."

"Oh, Amnon," she cried. "Don't be foolish! Don't do this to me! You know what a serious crime it is in Israel. Where could I go in my shame? And you would be called one of the greatest fools in Israel. Please, just speak to the king about it, for he will let you marry me. "But he wouldn't listen to her; and since he was stronger than she, he forced her. <u>Then suddenly his love turned to hate, and now he hated her more than he had loved her.</u>

"Get out of here!" he snarled at her.... So he put her out.

13

I will like to highlight a few points from this text;

1.   **Feelings appear real-** From the text above, we can see that Amnon had intense feelings for his half sister Tamar. The feeling was so strong that it made him feel really sick. It wasn't just an emotional effect, everyone could see it. If we could ask him, I am sure he would have described the feeling as something he had never felt before for any woman. He could not eat or drink, he had lost a lot of weight, all he could think about was his sister Tamar. Feelings can be that real and overwhelming. It changed everything about him.

2.   **Feelings control your actions-** One of the side effects of following your feelings is the fact that it lacks self-control. It can alter your behavior. This can be dangerous and have severe detrimental effects. Amnon, could not control his actions and ended up raping his half-sister Tamar. I have at several points in counseling gotten calls from individuals seeking counseling saying, "I am in love with so-and-so and I can't control myself around them. " That's not love. True love requires intentionality, so you are usually conscious of your actions.

3.   **Feelings are temporary-** After the act, the feeling of intense love gave way immediately to

intense hatred. Feelings always fade away after the excitement ends. It is not reliable, it is short-lived.

4. **Feelings unchecked have severe consequences**- I honestly wish I could tell single people this enough. A lot of singles have been wounded and battered because of their unchecked feelings. It isn't uncommon to hear reports like, "He is cheating on me, he abuses me emotionally, he spends my money irrationally but I can't leave him because of the feelings I have for him." This is totally unacceptable and it is not love. Many young people have lost their lives based on this. From our text, Amnon's uncontrolled feelings eventually led to his untimely death (2 Samuel 13:23-38).

So, love is not a feeling. Neither is it goosebumps or butterflies in your stomach. Love is not excitement about someone. All these are what the world wants you to believe that love is. Yes, there is a feeling part of love, but if it is genuine love, it will eventually grow into something more defined and real.

Love is a commitment; a pledge. It does not change based on how you feel or what is happening around you. When you say you love someone, it means you will stand by the person no matter the circumstances. The world has tried to define love based on feelings, but the only true definition of love can come from Love himself; God.

God's definition of love can be seen in 1 Corinthians 13: 4-8 (NKJV). It says –

"Love is patient, love is kind, it is not jealous; love does not brag, it is not arrogant. It does not act disgracefully, it does not seek its own benefit; it is not provoked, does not keep an account of a wrong suffered, it does not rejoice in unrighteousness, but rejoices with the truth; it keeps every confidence, it believes all things, hopes all things, endures all things. Love never fails; ..."

There is no 'feeling' mentioned in this scripture. Feelings will fizzle out sooner or later but the Bible says love never fails. This means you cannot stop loving someone when you commit to loving them. It is your commitment that keeps you going. Real love is sacrificial. We can see that clearly from John 3:16 (NLT);

For God so loved the world that he gave his one and only Son, that whoever believes in him shall not perish but have eternal life.

You can see from this verse that love gives sacrificially, the emphasis is on action and not feelings.

In the book of Ephesians 5:25-28 (NIV)

Husbands, love your wives, just as Christ loved the church and gave himself up for her to make her holy, cleansing her by the washing with water through the word, and to present her to himself as a radiant church, without stain or wrinkle or any other blemish, but holy and blameless.

In this same way, husbands ought to love their wives as their own bodies. He who loves his wife loves himself.

Yet again, no mention of feelings. I explained this in detail in my book, "The Three Kinds of Love Every Couple Needs".

Love can have feelings but in itself, it's not feelings. The danger of making love a feeling is that the day the feeling is not there, you will feel you are no more in love. This belief has made many couples give up on their marriages because they don't "feel" in love anymore. What they don't realize is the fact that feelings are never permanent. They are fickle by nature and so they fluctuate. We don't live by our feelings, we live by what the scripture says and the scripture says love is action.

Husbands, go all out in your love for your wives, exactly as Christ did for the church—a love marked by giving, not getting. Christ's love makes the church whole. His words evoke her beauty. Everything he

17

does and says is designed to bring the best out of her, dressing her in dazzling white silk, radiant with holiness. And that is how husbands ought to love their wives. They're really doing themselves a favor—since they're already "one" in marriage.
-Ephesians 5:25-29 [MSG]

The scripture says go all out. You should just keep doing what you do whether or not there is any change. Our feelings are directly influenced by our thoughts. Married couples need to understand that love has nothing to do with your feelings but everything to do with your commitment, so you should learn how to act in spite of how you feel. Like I always say, *It is easier to act your way into feeling than to feel your way into acting.* If you decide to take the right actions towards your spouse in practical things like being kind, tolerating them, giving them attention, surprises, etc. It would help your spouse understand what love truly is.

Another thing about feelings is that they are largely controlled by your thoughts. In other words, information affects affection. A while back, someone gave me some shirts as a gift but I left them in the gift bag for a long time because I had a lot of shirts already and had gotten weary of people giving me clothes. One day, I needed to go somewhere and was looking for a shirt to put on and then my wife brought out the gift bag and showed me the shirts that I had kept away and forgotten. I was reluctant to take a look at them but she encouraged me to try it on and when I did , I saw that I actually liked it. The fitting, the cut, the softness of the material, everything was on point!. It looked and felt very good on me.

I wanted more of it so I asked someone to help me find out how I could get more. I sent him the brand name and size. The person got back to me saying that the shirt cost 2000 Euros! I couldn't believe it! I had to ask him to check other stores outside Nigeria for it and he got back to me saying the same thing - The shirt cost over 2000 Euros. Immediately, my respect for the shirts increased and I started wearing them only on very special occasions because I now knew the worth and value. You see, I never liked the shirt before or even considered it important but the moment I got more information on the value of the shirt, my affection for it grew.

A lot of people that are quitting their marriages can actually feel love for their partners again if they work on it, and interestingly they can work on it. A few of the things that can help you rekindle your love life with your spouse are:

- Making sure you are not fixated on someone else because as long as you have another love interest, you won't "feel" love for your own partner.

- Refusing to dwell and focus on all the bad sides of your spouse.

- Feelings are also very selfish; it never considers the other party involved. Amnon thought he loved his half-sister, but he raped her. He never stopped to consider how his actions would hurt her. He only wanted to satisfy himself. When the feeling died after he raped her, he sent her away. Love is not selfish; love seeks not its own. Love always thinks of the other person. If Amnon really loved his half-sister, he would never have even thought of hurting her.

You can feel anger, hatred, jealousy, bitterness, happiness, pain, etc, but all these emotions never last, the feelings disappear when circumstances change. Love on the other hand cannot disappear no matter how much the circumstances change.

When Jesus was hanging on the cross and saw how the people He was dying for, mocked Him, if His love for us was just a feeling, I am so sure He would have said "I do not love these people anymore because they are mocking me". He stayed on the cross because he was committed to saving us from our sins, nothing changed that; not the strokes of the cane, not the spit from the mouths of those He was dying for that covered his face, not even the insults hurled at Him. Jesus loves us and He did not give up on His love for us. This is what love is, a commitment to stay with the person you have chosen regardless of the circumstances around you.

COMMON LOVE LIES

LIE 3

LOVE HAPPENS AT FIRST SIGHT

This is another lie made popular by romantic movies just to sell movie tickets. The truth is, romance and fantasy sells, the hope of magical love sells and of course the thought of living together happily ever after all sells. Now, it wouldn't be so bad if these thoughts weren't affecting us in real life. But from counselling feedback over the years, we can clearly see that they do. The media has sold us unrealistic love ideals.

A set of researchers set out in 2017 to study love at first sight as soon as it happened. They staged meetings with potential romantic partners for about 400 men and women and then asked about the feelings they experienced during the encounter. A small number of people did report falling in love at first sight, but those feelings didn't include high passion, intimacy, or commitment—all the classic hallmarks of romantics love psychologists look out for. The main factor that predicted falling in love at first sight with a stranger was physical attraction.

This suggests that a great majority of people who claim to have fallen in love at first sight are actually experiencing attraction at first sight.

Another research by the Wiley Online Library suggests that Love At First Sight (LAFS) is not a distinct form of love, but rather a strong initial attraction that some label as LAFS, either in the moment of first sight or retrospectively.

From these researches and several others, we can see that there is nothing like love at first sight. You can't truly love someone you don't know. What people call love at first sight is attraction at first sight, and that's quite normal. Usually when you meet someone, something will attract you to them, from surface things like their dressing, hairstyle or physical features to deeper things like their mind or spirituality but this doesn't mean it is love yet, it's attraction. You will need to know them better and build love over time.

If you will be sincere with yourself especially for those that are a bit mature, you will remember many times you thought you loved someone until you spent some time with them and discovered you couldn't really stand them. One of the reasons many people think it's love at first sight is because true love and fake love are somewhat identical at the beginning stages, they both come with some excitement until you give some time and the difference becomes clear. You can find some tips to knowing if you are truly loved in my book *"How to know if he/she really loves you"*. This will help open your eyes to truly know if your feelings for that person are fake or real.

"When I just saw you, I fell in love; I knew you were the one"...

This is a popular statement made popular in movies, that has been carried into real life. Love comes with such a serious responsibility that it cannot just emerge from first sight. Have you noticed that sometimes you can like something at first sight but later, you find out that it is not compatible with your life? Even Amnon did not love his sister at first sight; he had lived with her since they were children and only became more aware of her beauty as he observed and interacted with her daily until he became attracted to her.

If someone's appearance makes a huge impression on you when you see them for the first time, you are simply attracted to them. Love is such a deep commitment that is impossible to make at first sight. You can have attraction, infatuation or even erection at first sight but not love. Love is determined by some real and serious things like compatibility, friendship, kindness, etc and there's no way you can really determine these at first sight. So don't believe that it is love at first sight just because you are excited, take some time to know the person more before you commit.

Love never happens at first sight because love is a living thing; it grows. Love is a seed that must be planted, watered, and nurtured before it grows. When you meet someone for the first time and you like the person's character, or gestures, they become seeds in your heart that can grow into love if nurtured. The more you see the person and interact with the person, the more the love grows.

You can have attraction at first sight. What people call love at first sight is only a strong attraction that can grow into love with constant interaction with the person. Love and time work together; time usually exposes the true intentions of the heart and determines how deep your love goes for that person or thing. Without time, love cannot truly grow or take root. Love is built on knowledge and knowledge takes time to acquire. Love takes time and work to keep the fire burning and it takes commitment to keep that fire burning. Love at first sight is not pure love but only a strong attraction.

For instance, you can feel a strong attraction towards a Lamborghini or Ferrari, but when you begin to see the responsibilities attached to owning one, that attraction will slowly fade away. Or if you do not have a means to buy one, that attraction will either die or remain just an attraction. However, if you truly love the car, you will take a step further by making a commitment and buying the car. Some people buy the car before they even understand the responsibilities that go with it and when they find out, they become dissatisfied and either neglect the car or outrightly sell it. So, love at first sight is like buying a Lamborghini without complete knowledge of what goes into owning one. Knowledge strengthens love. It is very likely that if you get to know more about the person you think you love at first sight, you may begin to see things you do not even like and then the feeling disappears. Has that ever happened to you before? I'm sure it has, so its important to note that you can only love through knowledge and acquiring knowledge requires patience.

If you believe you really love someone, take time to get to know the person. Time is a true test of pure love. In 1st Corinthians 13, it says ';"Love is Patient". Patience is an attribute of time; if you truly love someone, you will be patient enough to wait and learn more about the person. Love is patient also means love waits for the right time. Love is never hurried. It is just like a seed; you need patience to keep watering and nurturing the seed until it begins to grow into something beautiful, something healthy and deeply rooted.

LIE 4

IF YOU LOVE ME, YOU WILL SLEEP WITH ME

This is a common lie that tricks people into premarital sex. Even though it has come to be almost acceptable, it is still a big fat lie. Sex and love are not related, at all. If sex was love then all the prostitutes walking the street would be in love. But we know that is not true, because there is no link between love and sex.

In our world today, young people are made to believe that sex is intimacy and so they have casual sex with multiple partners. Some others believe that sex builds intimacy, again this is not true. In fact, it's the other way round, it is intimacy that actually "builds" sex; makes sex better. Gottman's research has shown that a high quality friendship in a marriage is an important predictor in romantic and physical satisfaction. Couples that have good friendship and emotional connection have been found to enjoy sex better and for longer into their old age. So, keeping sex aside until marriage helps you focus on more important factors such as building friendship which is one factor that helps your marriage almost more than anything else.

One of the ways the devil has perverted love and marriage is through sex. People no longer see sex as something sacred and many people believe that everyone is having sex and so they feel comfortable in that lie and also do the same. This is not true. There are many people who live holy lives and remain virgins until they are married. I have been a pastor for more than twenty years, and I can tell you categorically that I have wedded quite a lot of virgins, that's the honest truth. Do not believe the lie that everybody is doing it.

Do not be deceived by anyone, true love will be willing to wait for you, true love will be willing to commit to marriage before sex. Lack of patience is a tell-tale sign that love is not present because 1st Corinthians 13 says love is PATIENT.

Love is patient and kind... I Corinthians 13:4a
[NLT]

True love gives and cares about the other person while lust seeks to take and cares only about self. Love thinks long term while lust is focused on the pleasure of the moment. Love is serious while lust is casual, love is special and rare while lust is common.

Don't believe the lie that love means sex, if it was so, everyone would be in love since everyone is having in sex. Sex is not the ultimate expression of love. If you ask married couples if sex is the only way they express love, they would tell you No. This is because there are a lot of other things that happen during the day and during the week that are a real test of their love, such as paying bills, taking care of their children, etc. Let's go back to the story of Amnon and Tamar. Amnon became so infatuated with his sister, he thought it was love. One of the reasons I am certain that Amnon did not truly love his sister is because the only way he was determined to express his love was through sex. One of the primary purposes of sex is pleasure and procreation and this is supposed to be within the confines of marriage. Sex is a beautiful gift from God and not a tool to prove whether or not a man or woman loves you.

God knew what He was doing when he asked us to keep the marriage bed undefiled. Let me tell you, people get tired of sex; ask couples who have been married for years. So, if you start having sex before marriage, chances are, you will get tired of sex faster when you get married. I have also seen virgins who were not able to have sex months into their marriage. However, with proper counselling, they were able to finally consummate the marriage. I have also wedded couples who complain to me that their wives do not have sex with them unless she wants to get pregnant, which is usually once in a year. Some women also complain that their husbands only touch them once in a year or never. Chances are that they have been sexually active before marriage. I

31

would rather be in the category of people who start having sex late and enjoy it well into my marriage than those who start having sex too early and get tired of it eventually. Once you start having sex before marriage, it corrupts your chances of true love.

Sex is a fuel that can help keep marriage going, but it should never be equated to love. When couples stop having sex, the flames of love will die, that's why people think love is sex. It is not, it is just a fuel to fan the flames of love.

A while ago, I began teaching a series I titled "Pink and Blue". The series explained the basic differences between men and women. One of the differences I mentioned is the fact that men can have sex with women they have no attachment to while it is usually harder for women to do so. Men do not necessarily need to feel any form of love or attraction towards the person they are having sex with. However, the reverse is the case for women as they usually would need to feel some sort of emotion towards a man before they have sex with him. And from previous chapters, we have established that this feeling does not necessarily have to be love.

If sex was love, we would not have prostitutes on the street; they are there simply to satisfy the physical pleasures of men. Sex outside of marriage is simply sex but in marriage it can be an expression of love. If you truly love someone, your first thought should not be to have sex with the person. That's a user's mentality. You just want to use them to satisfy your uncontrolled passion. So, from this I'm sure you now know that anyone who asks you to prove your love for them with sex does not genuinely love you. That individual is looking for someone they can use to satisfy their sexual desires with and this is selfish.

Love is not ill-mannered or selfish or irritable; love does not keep a record of wrongs;
1st Corinthians 13:5[GNT]

Even married couples know that there are a lot of other ways they express love to each other which does not necessarily involve sex. Sometimes sex does not even happen for days but couples still love each other. There are also couples who do not love each other but still have sex; this is because it is a basic need that all humans have whether you are in love or not.

Love and sex are two completely different things and should never be compared to each other.

LIE 5

YOU CAN BUY LOVE WITH MONEY OR MATERIAL THINGS

When we were young, there were lots of songs that made it clear that money cannot buy "true" love. But, it seems with time that the music has not only changed in favour of money, it has also changed the narrative of relationships. These days, most music videos show a male figure with expensive cars, jewellery and money being surrounded by a lot of women. Somehow, people have come to think or believe that if you are rich enough or can throw money around a lot, you can find love. I'm sorry to disappoint you but that won't happen.

Money definitely can buy sex. It may even buy someone's seeming loyalty but it will never buy true love! And this can be seen in Songs of Solomon 8:7,

Love cannot be drowned by oceans or floods. It cannot be bought--any offer would be scorned no matter how great.
- Songs of Solomon 8:7 [CEV]

35

I get questions along these lines a lot and most times these questions are disheartening. I remember getting a question from a young man during one of our conferences who said, he had a lady he loved, he bought her lots of gifts and gave her lots of money and still she didn't love him, his question was, "what should he do?" I am not sure I will ever fully understand the later part of that question- "what should he do?" What are the options really? Kidnap her and force her to marry you? Of course not! You can't force someone to love you, that's selfish. So move on.

I tell single people all the time that love is not a trade commodity; you can neither buy nor sell it. If you give everything you have for love, no matter how expensive, those things will be despised. So many people enter relationships and they are the only ones giving. They give their time, money, attention and body hoping to win over the affection of the person they love. The truth, however is, if a person does not love you, there is nothing you can do or give that will make them love you. They might receive your gifts and take undue advantage of you but they will never be truly committed to you. Real love demands commitment from both parties. No matter how much you give someone in order to win their love, there will always be someone who would be willing to give even more. And guess what? If the person you think you have bought with gifts finds someone who is ready to shower even more on them, they will walk away without looking back.

You see, humans are quite deep. Actually much deeper than you think. Yes, on the surface you may influence people with your money but the truth is it never lasts. I see this a lot during counselling sessions. It might even interest you to know that as of 2020, nine out of the ten richest men in the world are divorced. If anyone could buy love it would be these men. Money can dazzle for a short time but after a while, the person's heart will crave a real connection. You see, as humans we have three parts - spirit, soul and body. Material things can only benefit physically but usually cannot benefit the soul and spirit, so no amount of material gifts will make someone that doesn't want you, genuinely love you. You can actually woo people with what you have but in the end they have to see more meaning into you than the material things you have given them. They should be able to buy into you as a person and love you to the point that even though you don't have those things anymore, they would still love you. Material things only entice the mind for a short while and cannot be used to buy someone's love. You can use it to get someone's attention but definitely not love. In the end, the person you are lavishing with money or gifts will fall in love with your money and gifts, once they stop coming, the person's attitude will change towards you.

Now, one thing a lot of women need to understand is this, if you marry a man because of his material possessions, he will treat you like one of his material possessions. He will love you the way he loves his car, house or even the furniture in his house. Just as men change cars when they get bored with one, they will get a new model when they get bored with you.

Proverbs 31:10 says, *"Who can find a virtuous woman? For her price is far above rubies"*

The Bible describes a virtuous woman as being priceless, and this is how you should see yourself as a woman. No material thing is worth your time or heart. If you can live with the consciousness of what you are worth, no one will be able to entice you with material things. Your price is far above rubies. Rubies are very rare gemstones and after they have been refined, can be more expensive than diamonds and the Bible says your price is far above rubies.

People who equate material things with love mostly have a self esteem problem. If you know who you are and what you are worth, material things will not entice you. If you feel the need to buy people's love, you do not know your worth. Likewise, if you love someone because of the gifts the person gives you, you also do not know who you are and what you are worth.

You are worth so much more than you are selling yourself. The Bible says,

Because you are precious in My sight and honored, and because I love you, I will give men in return for you and peoples in exchange for your life.
- Isaiah 43:4[AMPC]

God did not say this just to get you excited, He actually gave up His only Son for you because you are extremely valuable and precious in His sight.

If God didn't hesitate to put everything on the line for us, embracing our condition and exposing himself to the worst by sending his own Son, is there anything else he wouldn't gladly and freely do for us?   *- Romans 8 :32 [MSG]*

The great price God paid for you is the life of His Son, Jesus. You are worth dying for. Do not let anyone belittle you and buy you with material things that will not last. And, don't put yourself in a position where you are simply managed because of what you can provide.

LIE 6

YOU DON'T CHOOSE
WHO YOU LOVE,
LOVE CHOOSES YOU.

I have heard a lot of people give this as an excuse to cheat or as an escape from the real commitments of marriage, but it is a lie. You can choose who you love and who you will not love. Love does not jump on anyone, it is a choice. A deliberate one at that. Just like I have mentioned several times in preceding chapters, we have no idea how much movies, music and literature, especially romance novels, have impacted how we see love.

The idea of love choosing you, I believe, was birthed by the mythical cupid. He was thought to be the Roman god of love and was prominent for appearing with a bow and a quiver of arrows whose wounds inspired love or passion in its victims. Over time, more and more people have come to accept this but it is a lie. You hear them say things like, "Cupid has shot his arrow through my heart" meaning they are lovestruck, smitten by love or head-over-heels in love with someone. The belief is, once that arrow touches you, you have no choice but to fall in love and all of this is not true!

In fact, a lot of people still believe they don't choose who they love and this has put them in difficult and toxic situations regarding their relationships and marriages. I also believe this is where the term "falling in love" emanated from. Well, from what I know, falling has always been a dangerous and harmful experience. People get hurt when they fall. And, that is the reason God didn't create us to fall in love but rather to grow in love. The former is involuntary, emotional and unpredictable while the latter is voluntary, intentional and predictable and that's how true love is and should be.

When people claim to fall in love, they are also saying they are not responsible for their actions or emotions. They use phrases like, "I just love you and I don't know why." I know this sounds romantic to some people but what it truly means is that they can equally say, "I hate you and don't know why". You see, falling in love is purely emotional but growing in love is intentional. Our emotions are fickle, it's never stable, so you can't build a real relationship or marriage on it. You can be attracted to someone but that's not love. In fact, everytime you lose control of your senses and behaviour, it's a telltale sign that it's not love; true love is a decision, a commitment to stand by someone in spite of how you feel.

The Bible actually expects us to consciously choose who we love and then make a commitment to love them. When it comes to true love, you can choose where to set your affections.

Set your affection on things above,
not on things on the earth.

- Colossians 3:2 [KJV]

Jesus said to him, "'You shall love the LORD your God with all your heart, with all your soul, and with all your mind.'

- Matthew 22:37 [NKJV]

The texts above make it clear that you can and in fact, should choose who you love and not just fall in love. Another way to look at it is that the Bible never said to marry who you love but to love who you marry. This means love is a decision you can make at any point in the equation. Most people like the idea that they are not in control of their emotions but it is not scriptural, neither does it make sense. In every country with law and order, people are penalised or arrested when they drive under the influence of certain substances. The reason is simply that they are no longer in control and as such, they are a threat or danger not only to themselves but to others.

So, love is a conscious decision you have to make and with this decision comes responsibilities and a commitment to fulfil those responsibilities no matter the circumstance. Saying you don't choose who you love gives the impression that you were not in control of your senses when you got into that relationship and that's totally irresponsible. Over time, I have observed that when it comes to love, people constantly try not to take responsibility for their actions. They'd rather blame their emotions for their actions. Just to help you understand this better, if love "chooses" you and a deranged person, would you go ahead saying you can't help it? Of course you won't. It's the same with any other toxic relationship situation. So you can choose not to love that married man, you can choose not to love that guy who constantly belittles you, you can choose not to love people you have no business being with. Love is not a trap; it does not draw you in and then lock you up.

Love is a lifelong commitment that requires your conscious investment. Think about it, when choosing a school for your children do you just pick any school that sends you a proposal? How about choosing a car to buy, do you just pick one because the sales person tells you it's a great deal? Don't you weigh the pros and cons of buying that particular car? How much more, your choice of a life partner; don't you think you should make the choice of someone you would spend the rest of your life with? Don't you think it should be well thought out?

Listen, if a man or woman tells you they do not know why they love you, you are in a dangerous relationship that will only end badly because one day that same person will say they no longer love you and not know why. I know why I love my wife and every day I am reminded why. These reasons keep me in the marriage, no matter what happens.

So love is a decision, and you can choose to make it a right decision.

LIE 7

I CAN LOVE MORE THAN ONE PERSON

I once heard a song with the lyrics, 'I'm in love with two women, I don't know which one to choose...' Well, if you are describing love as an emotion or attraction then yes, you can be attracted to not only two but a thousand people. A good example is King Solomon in the Bible (1st Kings 11:3). He had seven hundred wives and three hundred concubines. Can you imagine that? Can you imagine the time, effort and resources he would have to invest into all these relationships?

The truth is, you can have an emotional connection with more than one person but you cannot love more than one person, because love by its definition and nature is <u>loyal</u> and <u>committed</u>. According to Oxford Languages, being loyal refers to giving or showing firm and constant support or <u>allegiance</u> to a person, while Dictionary.com defines commitment as being bound or obligated to a person or thing, as by pledge or assurance; devoted.

An article published by Libretext Social sciences on loving more than one person at the same time within the context of romantic relationships reveals that, "loving more than one person at a time in terms of participating in a fully loving — including a fully and mutually benevolent, and fully and mutually satisfying relationship — it is practically impossible to have a romantic loving relationship with more than one person at a time." When people say they love two or more people at the same time, what they are talking about is lust. These same people, if tables were turned, would die of a heartbreak if they found out that their partners also had two or more love affairs at the same time. No one wants to be an option or a side piece. So, true love demands loyalty and faithfulness, commitment and dedication to a single individual.

When people say that they are in love with more than one person, what they really mean is that they are attracted to more than one person. Attraction is something that can happen to anyone, even a married person can be attracted to someone else, but you cannot be in love with two people. So, how do you differentiate love from attraction? Knowledge. A good knowledge of these individuals will show you who you are attracted to and who you are in love with. Attraction is usually not based on knowledge. It is usually just on the surface; you can be attracted to a smile, the way someone dresses, the way someone laughs or any other pleasant attribute they possess but love is usually deeper and requires commitment.

I usually tell people that commitment to your spouse is like buying a DSTV with the option of hundreds of interesting channels and choosing to watch only one for the rest of your life. That's a huge sacrifice. This is because there will always be people you will find attractive for one reason or the other but true love demands leaving all others and ensuring undivided commitment to your spouse, alone. Love in its truest form is single-minded. The Bible says,

""No one can serve two masters. Either you will hate the one and love the other, or you will be devoted to the one and despise the other. You cannot serve both God and money."

Matthew 6:24. [NIV]

I have seen singles who are confused because they think they are in love with two people and can't decide who to choose. I get such calls so frequently. You'd hear them say, "I am in love with Jane and Joan, I can't decide who to be with." Interestingly, I addressed that clearly in one of my books, *"Who Should I Marry?"* I itemised specific attributes you should look out for at such times. So, if you take time to get to know these two people, you will find out that you are only attracted to one of them and will be able to recognize the person you truly love.

Once you have decided to love someone and be with that person, every other form of affection must be treated as nothing but an attraction that will eventually run its course and fade away due to lack of commitment. Never forget, commitment means your singular focus is on one person and that is what true love is all about.

LIE 8

LOVE MUST BE CRAZY, EXCITING AND MAKE ME LOSE MY SENSES

Love is not senseless or crazy. If anything, love is one of the most intentional and calculated human experiences. Yes, love is exciting and can be adventurous but it demands conscious efforts to make it work. The idea that love is crazy was gotten from movies and music. Another effect I must blame on the existence of Hollywood, Bollywood and Nollywood. We feel there must be butterflies in our tummies, we must have lovestruck eyes, we become distracted and forgetful, with wandering minds, and unrealistic imaginations. All these events sometimes happen but don't always have to be so. Love can also be cool, calm and calculated.

My love for Pastor Mildred was not crazy at all, it was more calculated than anything else. I knew what I wanted, saw it and went for it. It was exciting but I never lost my senses. In fact, we both agreed that if we felt at any point that we were not sure of our decision to be together, we would stop the process, even if it's on the wedding day. We were very much in our senses.

A lot of single people have crazy experiences which they attribute to love. Things like forgetfulness, distractions, physiological changes amongst other symptoms. All these are not signs of love. Some have serious fights when planning their wedding, ours was very calm and peaceful. We agreed on everything, no drama at all, we weren't losing our heads and all the other funny things people say.because of love So, love doesn't have to be crazy to be love.

Let's take a look at a story in the book of Judges 16:4-22(MSG) that drives this home better.

Some time later he fell in love with a woman in the Valley of Sorek (Grapes). Her name was Delilah. The Philistine tyrants approached her and said, "Seduce him. Discover what's behind his great strength and how we can tie him up and humble him. Each man's company will give you a hundred shekels of silver."

So Delilah said to Samson, "Tell me, dear, the secret of your great strength, and how you can be tied up and humbled."

Samson told her, "If they were to tie me up with

*seven bowstrings—the kind made from fresh animal
tendons, not dried out—then I would become weak,
just like anyone else."*

*The Philistine tyrants brought her seven bowstrings,
not dried out, and she tied him up with them. The
men were waiting in ambush in her room. Then she
said, "The Philistines are on you, Samson!" He
snapped the cords as though they were mere threads.
The secret of his strength was still a secret.*

*Delilah said, "Come now, Samson—you're playing
with me, making up stories. Be serious; tell me how
you can be tied up."*

*He told her, "If you were to tie me up tight with new
ropes, ropes never used for work, then I would be
helpless, just like anybody else."*

*So Delilah got some new ropes and tied him up. She
said, "The Philistines are on you, Samson!" The
men were hidden in the next room. He snapped the
ropes from his arms like threads.*

*Delilah said to Samson, "You're still playing games
with me, teasing me with lies. Tell me how you can
be tied up."*

*He said to her, "If you wove the seven braids of my
hair into the fabric on the loom and drew it tight,*

then I would be as helpless as any other mortal."

When she had him fast asleep, Delilah took the seven braids of his hair and wove them into the fabric on the loom and drew it tight. Then she said, "The Philistines are on you, Samson!" He woke from his sleep and ripped loose from both the loom and fabric!

She said, "How can you say 'I love you' when you won't even trust me? Three times now you've toyed with me, like a cat with a mouse, refusing to tell me the secret of your great strength."

She kept at it day after day, nagging and tormenting him. Finally, he was fed up—he couldn't take another minute of it. He spilled it.

He told her, "A razor has never touched my head. I've been God's Nazirite from conception. If I were shaved, my strength would leave me; I would be as helpless as any other mortal."

When Delilah realized that he had told her his secret, she sent for the Philistine tyrants, telling them, "Come quickly—this time he's told me the truth." They came, bringing the bribe money.

When she got him to sleep, his head on her lap, she motioned to a man to cut off the seven braids of his hair. Immediately he began to grow weak. His strength drained from him.

*Then she said, "The Philistines are on you, Samson!"
He woke up, thinking, "I'll go out, like always, and
shake free." He didn't realize that God had
abandoned him.*

*The Philistines grabbed him, gouged out his eyes, and
took him down to Gaza. They shackled him in irons
and put him to the work of grinding in the prison..."*

Samson was a judge in his time. He was a warrior and
leader at the same time but senseless love brought an
end to everything he was designed to achieve. It's the
same with most people today when they say they are
in love, you'd find doctors, lawyers, security
personnel, leaders who literally throw away all their
sense of judgement because of love. We've had cases
of strong leaders who could not be brought down by
top security personnels but were brought down in a
few hours by crazy love.

Think about it, Delilah asked Samson the source of
his strength several times and each time he gave her a
clue, she acted on it quickly and called out to him
that soldiers were attacking him. Logically, if he
wasn't so "crazily in love", and she had been acting
on every false tip he gave her, why would he still give
her the right secret knowing that she would act on
it? That's what crazy love does, it's senseless and
reckless.

I know there are certain schools of thought and research that say that a person in love is a person with impaired judgement. That the area of the brain associated with judgement stops working when someone is in love which can make people do crazy things because they are not making logical decisions. They may do things that are unsafe or over the top. They may find themselves making choices that they wouldn't make normally. That doesn't have to be you. As believers, we can make smart love decisions. Let's see the scripture below;

I pray that your love will keep on growing more and more, together with true knowledge and <u>perfect judgment,</u>

Philippians 1:0[GNT]

See, you can actually make perfect judgement when you are in love. And even though love influences your actions, you can choose not to act impulsively. You have self-control. So, your love based decisions should be smart not senseless. Here's a prayer for you;

So this is my prayer: that your love will flourish and that you will not only love much but well. Learn to <u>love appropriately</u>. You need to use <u>your head and</u>

test your feelings so that your love is sincere and intelligent, not sentimental gush.
Philippians 1:9[MSG]

And this is my prayer for you as well that you will learn to love appropriately and intelligently.

LIE 9

LOVE IS A CURE FOR INDISCIPLINE

Some people think, "if I love my spouse I won't be attracted to another person". This belief is what makes people let down their guard and often slack in their responsibilities. They think if they're in love they're safe. They assume people in love can't cheat or be attracted to someone else but hey, that's not true.

A study published in the *Journal of Sex and Marital Therapy, had* almost 70% of participants who said they had experienced some kind of attraction toward someone other than their spouse while in a long-term relationship. This was observed even amongst happy, committed, monogamous relationships. Another study conducted by the University of Vermont revealed that 98% of men and 80% of women have fantasised about someone other than their current spouses. The truth is, all through your life you will see people you are attracted to. You will actually see qualities in other people that are not present in your spouse that gets your attention. They can be physical qualities like beauty, shape, fitness, handsomeness or even spiritual qualities. I mean, a wide variety of things can cause someone to stray, so the determining factor is not whether you will get attracted but what you do about it. What stops us from straying or cheating is not love but discipline and boundaries.

Some people believe that once they find someone they love; they will never be tempted to cheat or will never look at another man or woman again. They believe that once you find someone you love; every other feeling dies. Unfortunately, this is not true, love does not automatically stop you from being attracted to other people. If love is a cure for indiscipline, there will be no cases of infidelity in marriages.

There are also people who believe that once they fall in love, everything will change; they will stop looking at other women or men, they will be wiser in spending money, they will be better managers of time, etc. However, this too is not true, the only cure for indiscipline is to work on your mind, and be deliberate about the decisions you make. Love will not cure any of these things, especially infidelity.

You will still be attracted to many other people when you get married; however, the most important thing is what you choose to do with the attraction when it happens. Will you act on it or remember the commitment you have made to your spouse? Discipline is a choice you make as a result of love, it will not happen automatically. You have to make the decision deliberately not to cheat on your spouse or act on an attraction you feel towards someone else.

Sometimes, this is not easy especially if the object of your attraction is someone you are in close proximity to. However, it is not an impossible situation. The thing about commitment is it should make you accountable to your spouse or fiancé. Commitment means you do not keep secrets from your spouse, you give your all to this one person. If you find yourself being attracted to someone else, tell your spouse. Love is like a shield that protects two people, but if you do not activate it by being open with your spouse, you will find yourself being unfaithful.

Love will not stop you from getting attracted to other people, but love is strong enough to keep you from acting on that attraction. One of the attributes of love mentioned in 1 Corinthians 13:6 (NIV) is, *"Love does not delight in evil but rejoices with the truth."*

Yielding to any other attraction outside the one you have for your spouse is wrong. When you love someone, you do not purposely hurt them. Aligning to the truth of God's word and staying faithful to your spouse is key to successful relationships. You constantly choose to make this person happy, to stay true to this one person. This is the truth that must motivate the decisions you make in your marriage or relationship.

The Bible also says in John 8:32, "And you shall know the truth and the truth shall make you free". If you hold on to this truth, it will set you free.

LIE 10

THERE WILL BE NO CHALLENGES OR DOUBTS IN YOUR HEART WHEN THERE IS LOVE.

Love does not automatically stop you from facing challenges or having doubts in your marriage or relationships. Some people believe that when there is true love, everything will be perfect; you'll end each other's sentences, read each other's minds, suddenly have passion for the same things, and so on. These things are only realities in movies and novels, not in the real world. Even when you are in love, there will be challenges.

Interestingly, you don't choose the challenges you will face as a couple. But, you can choose to be on the same team irrespective of the challenges. Your bond of commitment to each other must be intact. The truth is, the devil hates love and marriage and will do everything in his power to destroy it. You may not have challenges when you are just friends, but the moment you make a commitment to love each other, the devil begins to attack. Your greatest weapon at this time would be your commitment to each other. Sadly, a lot of couples begin to point fingers and blame one another for their misfortune. I have heard cases where immediately after the marriage, the man loses his job and puts the blame on his wife saying, since she came into his life everything has gone bad; no promotion, no business deals and no money. You need to realise that she is not to blame. In fact, according to scripture, she is the one who brings favour into your life. If you fight her, you are only fighting off favour from your life and your prayers would be hindered. Instead of playing the blame game, leverage on the power of agreement and stand on the Word of God together and you will see the tides change in favour of your union.

The true test of love is your commitment to each other. If you run or give up in the face of trials and temptations then you need to work on your love. When I counsel couples whose parents refuse to give consent for their marriage; the first question I ask them is "What are both of you saying concerning this?" If they are both in agreement and are committed to making things work, every other factor does not matter that much anymore. I am usually more interested in what the individuals in question are saying. If both of them are committed, then they can find a way around it. If one of the parties is not committed or in doubt, there is nothing anyone can do to help them. They must both speak in unity.

When I was going to get married to my wife, my in-laws did not think it was a good idea. I was always visiting her and her father noticed my constant presence in their house. So, one day he summoned me and asked me what my intentions were toward his daughter. I knew this would be my only chance to make my intentions known to him. So I told him I wanted to marry his daughter and he said it was impossible. My wife told me not to worry and that was all that mattered to me, what her father said did not matter so much anymore because I was assured of her commitment to me. A short while after, we started taking active steps together; we spoke to her siblings first and then they spoke to their parents who later agreed to the marriage. Today, everyone involved is happy.

The Bible says in Matthew 18:19, "Again I say to you, that if two of you agree on earth about anything that they may ask, it shall be done for them by My Father who is in heaven". Listen, there is power in two people being committed to each other and being in agreement. When people use parental consent as an excuse not to get married, it just shows their level of commitment to each other.

Being in love does not mean that you will not have challenges, what matters is that the two of you are committed. If you are committed there is nothing you cannot go through and win. Remember the story of the tower of Babel? As long as they were together, as long as they spoke one language, they were undefeatable and indivisible so much that God even agreed that nothing could stop them.

"But the LORD came down to look at the city and the tower the people were building. "Look!" he said. "The people are united, and they all speak the same language. After this, nothing they set out to do will be impossible for them!"

- Genesis 11:5-6 [NLT]

LIE 11

LOVE IS ENOUGH

I can't tell you how many times I have heard this love lie, even from well meaning loved ones and family members. They'd tell you, "as long as you love each other deeply, you will be fine". This is a lie, a devastating one at that. Many people come to realise after a while, either during their courtship or in marriage that there's more to marital success than just being in love- there is work involved!

A lot of people believe you do not need to do any work to make love work. They think that once it is true love, it will flow and work naturally, some others feel once you are in love, you will always be in love. It sounds good to the ears but it is not true. As powerful as love is, it needs to be serviced. Love does not grow naturally; it is not automatic. You need to put in the work to make it grow stronger. Love is not a robot that you just put on and then it does all the work itself, love is manual labour, you have to work it out yourself.

This is why it is important to know why you love someone because that is the fuel that will keep the flame burning. I know why I love my wife and every day I am reminded of it. You must know why you love someone; it is very important as it will serve as a reminder to you putting in the work. A marriage needs way more than the feeling of love to work and couples need to always be reminded of this because oftentimes in counselling, I hear the men say, "I have done everything to show her that I love her yet she says I don't love her". On the other hand, women also talk about how they have tried to be the "perfect" wife, serving and respecting their husbands but still he says she does not respect him.

I often tell people, if you want a successful marriage don't read only marriage books, read financial books, spiritual development books, books on communication, etc. There are other factors that determine whether a marriage will work or not such as financial management, sex, communication, and respect which is very important for men. A man desperately needs respect. In fact, most men will consider leaving a home where they are not respected. So loving your spouse is like buying a car or a generator, constantly servicing it is required to keep it working efficiently. When Jesus died for our sins, He did not return to heaven, cross His legs and then watch His sacrifice of love continue naturally. He gave us the Holy Spirit to keep the fire burning in our hearts every day. Our constant communion with the Holy Spirit is what keeps our love for Jesus alive. If Jesus had returned to heaven and left us here without the Holy Spirit to keep his love in our hearts alive, Christianity may have long gone into extinction.

Listen, when you meet someone for the first time and you know that you love this person, there are several things you do to show how much you love them; you go out on dates, you buy each other gifts, tell each other "I love you" as much as possible, etc. All these gestures are fuel that fan the flames of love and you must continue to do them even after you are married.

Many marriages grow cold after a few years and the couples are quick to think they are no more in love with each other. This is usually not the case, if they begin to deliberately do the things they used to do when they first met such as making constant phone calls, depositing words of kindness, showing appreciation, forgiving one another, etc; their love will be rekindled. If you do not feel like you love your partner anymore, I challenge you to begin to take deliberate steps to service your love and you will begin to see changes. Look at what the Bible says:

However, I have this against you: The love you had at first is gone.
- Revelations 2:4 [GWT]

This scripture acknowledges that there was once love but steps to ensure the love grew weren't put in place. The truth is, love can grow and love can die. So you and your spouse should be intentional about keeping your love alive. Acts such as being kind to each other, being conscious of the way you speak to your spouse, showing etiquette, going out on dates, appreciating little actions, affirming your spouse, etc. My wife and I have a book called *"All Year Round for Men"* and *"All Year Round for Women"* which gives you coaching tips from us on how to show love to your spouse every week, all through the year. We have recorded so many testimonies from these books because for the first time people find simple and practical ways to actively grow the love relationship between them and their spouses.

Love is like an investment; the more work you put into it, the more joy you will get out of it and like I always say, "you harvest where you invest". You need to continuously make investments and sacrifices when it comes to growing the love you have for your partner. It will not happen automatically. Love is very demanding; it will demand your time, resources, your heart, it will demand everything from you and you must be willing to give it your all if you want to enjoy your life. If you are not willing to make this sacrifice, then you are not ready for love.

Another notion similar to this is that people think that **true love never dies.** They think that if they have true love it will always survive no matter what. This is not true. If you continue to treat your spouse wrongly, the love they have for you will eventually die. Besides if something can grow then it can also die.

I've been married to my wife for almost 18 years and to be honest, it doesn't feel like that at all. It just feels like 8 months. I can say categorically that I literally love my wife more now than when I first met her. I didn't know that was possible but you see, love can actually grow. Some other people in 18 years will be talking about how much their spouse disgusts them and wonder how they got into the relationship in the first place, they would begin to consider getting a new spouse. You need to be intentional about doing the things that would make both of you remain in love.

Love doesn't automatically stay alive, it has to be kept alive.

LIE 12

THERE IS NOTHING LIKE TRUE LOVE

This lie comes mainly from hurt and disappointed people who are speaking from their experience. Truly, breakups are painful but do not make definite conclusions because of your bad experiences, true love exists and you can experience it. The Bible says so, data supports it, I also can categorically say that I am experiencing it. There is true love! The only issue is that there's so much lack of knowledge about love and relationships, so people are getting heart broken and they feel no one is having a good experience.

Of all the lies people believe about love, this is the one that bothers me the most because this is what the devil wants people to believe; if he can get people to believe less in love, he can destroy the foundation of marriage. The devil hates marriage. This is why it is always under heavy attack and one of the reasons is that; he does not want God to have "Godly seed".

Has not the one God made you? You belong to him in body and spirit. And what does the one God

73

seek? Godly offspring. So be on your guard, and do not be unfaithful to the wife of your youth.

- Malachi 2:15 [NIV]

This is what the devil is fighting, - raising more godly seeds. When people stop believing in love, they will most likely not get married and therefore will not have children (godly seed). This is why marriage has become so perverted with the Lesbian, Gay, Bisexual, Transgender & Queer movement. (LGBTQ). The devil hates marriage and will do anything to prevent happy marriages especially amongst Christians because they will teach their children about God.

Listen, true love exists. Not just in fairy tales and novels, it exists in reality. It is possible for two people to love each other and be committed to each other. It is possible to have a marriage void of cheating, fighting or abuse. Despite all the divorces you hear about and all the bad marriages that you see or read about, there are still a lot of good marriages. You must understand that generally, bad news is more publicized than good news but do not be deceived, there are also great marriages that are not being publicized. There are many marriages that are stress-free, fight-free, quarrel-free, no abusive words and the couples genuinely love each other and constantly work towards pleasing each other every single day. The devil will try to tell you that there is no true love, listen, there is true love; and, it is very important that you know this.

The devil is always seeking ways to deceive people and make them believe that it is okay to have a horrible marriage and you have to just manage what you get. I once spoke to a lady who said while she was in the university, her roommates were discussing marriage and they all said it is not possible for a man to remain faithful to one woman and they are okay with it as long as he does not bring the other woman into their matrimonial homes. She said she was shocked and told them that it was a lie and she would marry a man that would be faithful to her. They laughed at her, but today, she is married to a godly man who is very faithful to her and they both got married as virgins. This is a very sad and wrong mindset to have about love and marriage. Do not be deceived, you can have a marriage filled with pure and true love. This is very important; True love is very real and you can enjoy it in your marriage. However, you must be willing to do the right things to enjoy true love.

LIE 13

LOVE WILL CHANGE ME

Love is very powerful, but it is not powerful enough to change your bad character. Some people believe once they get married, love will change them; they will no longer be rude, they will be more humble, more homely, etc. This is a lie and this is where people get into trouble; they leave the responsibility of change to love.

Let me tell you right away, the person you were before marriage is the same person you will be in marriage if you don't work on yourself. Someone once said, "there is no problem with marriage; the real problem is when people enter into a marriage with all their bad character and then turn the marriage into a problematic one." And, this is so true. Marriage in itself is not bad, it simply takes on the character of the people involved in it.

Many people get married with the hopes that love will miraculously change all their bad behaviour and this usually does not happen automatically. If you get married with a bad attitude you will corrupt your marriage with your bad attitude. You need to work on yourself before you get married. If you have unresolved issues in your heart or with your past, love will not make them disappear. Women are usually victims of this lie; they believe the love they have for a guy will make him change. When they eventually get married, many years down the line, they discover the man is still a liar, a cheat, and still abusive. Love cannot automatically change bad character, only the Holy Spirit can do that and that is achieved through prayers and strong convictions not love.

What love can do is to help you bear the pain that will come as a result of bad attitudes, love can help you forgive a cheating partner, love can give you patience to deal with the excesses of an irresponsible partner but love will not change them neither will it change you. You need to change your mindset and make the right choices before marriage, do not be blinded by love. Work on yourself if you have character flaws you know will be a problem when you get married or when you are in a relationship. My advice is that you get help or counselling to deal with all your unresolved issues before you even think of falling in love.

LIE 14

NOBODY LOVES ME

This is one lie that the devil has been propagating for many generations and it becomes very rampant when there are celebrations or holidays like Valentine's day or Christmas. People begin to feel unloved either because they don't have a date or because they didn't get any gifts. At times like this, the tendency is high for most people to begin to think that they are not loved because they did not receive the desires of their hearts. I need you to see this lie for what it really is: an attempt to make you forget that you are a child of God and God has no unloved children. It is a lie because as a child of God you are loved. You are truly loved! And loved by the most powerful being - God. See what the Bible says about you-

For God so loved the world, that he gave his only begotten Son, that whosoever believeth in him should not perish, but have everlasting life.

- John 3:16 [KJV]

As the Father has loved Me, so have I loved you. Remain in My love.
- John 15:9[BSB]

Did you see that scripture? I love it. Jesus was saying that as the Father has loved him, so has He loved you. Even if you feel there's nobody that loves you in this world, I'm here to introduce someone to you today that loves you. Jesus said, "I love you". I mean, is that not music to your ears? I know how ladies like to hear those three magical words. Some guys do too, but guess what? God has told you the same words, "I love you". So settle it once and for all, you are loved. Every child of God is loved. Don't believe the lie that you are not loved. Don't get into a sad mood or allow yourself to become depressed.

I know that with the advent of social media it has become more difficult to ignore the need for a physical human being's expression of love especially because you will see so many people displaying their affection online and in very extravagant ways. Listen, If you need to stay off social media sometimes, please do. Most people actually need to grow when it comes to managing their emotions to the point where their joy remains intact when others flag or advertise their own joy. Just because somebody is posting their joy shouldn't take away your own joy. I say this because there are so many people that are so affected by the testimony and joys of others. So, if somebody posts their wedding picture, new car, new house, or any other thing that they find joy in, don't begin to pity yourself and please don't lose your joy.

You are loved and the beautiful thing about the kind of love that God gives is that it is more precious, valuable, solid and stable than the one human beings have to offer or the one people are posting online. So don't allow anyone to make you feel inferior.

Greater love has no one than this, that he lay down his life for his friends.

- John 15:13 [BSB]

The greatest way to show love for friends   is to die for them.

- John 15:13 (CEV)

There are different kinds of love but none is greater than the love Jesus has for you. The scriptures above make this clear. A love that lays down one's life for his friends; that is what Jesus did for you. So many times when a man wants to get a woman to marry him, part of his lines would include, "I would die for you..." but here we find a love that is not only saying that but has done that - Jesus actually died for you! Open up to the love of Christ. Experiencing the love of Christ will help you set your love standards right. You will be able to determine what you can accept and what you can't accept when it comes to loving someone and being loved.

so that Christ may dwell in your hearts through faith. And I pray that you, being rooted and established in love.

- Ephesians 3:17 [NIV]

The reason we have not been able to appreciate the love of God is because we are always comparing it to the natural love we have around us. This is why you can't envy anybody that is even in love today because some of those love escapades are seasonal, they start on February 1st and end after Valentine's day- a touch and go kind of love or a here today gone tomorrow kind of love.

The love of God is greater than the love from any human being. Infact, God expects us to approach human love already full of His love. That's the best way to handle human love.

May be able to comprehend with all saints what is the breadth, and length, and depth, and height;

- Ephesians 3:18 [KJV]

This is so powerful! Many people are sad and depressed because they are trying to build their lives on human love. Human love is good but it is not the best.

And to know the love of Christ, which passeth
knowledge, that ye might be filled with all the
fulness of God.

- Ephesians 3:19 [KJV]

I saw a post from someone I follow on social media recently. She said she did not know that God could answer a "stupid" prayer. This amazed me because I couldn't believe that some people actually think they are disturbing God when they pray to Him for seemingly 'unimportant' things! God loves you so much, you literally can't disturb Him about anything that concerns you. Do you know God knows the number of hair on your head? He numbered them. He knows the exact number that falls when you go to get a haircut at the salon and look where it gets even more beautiful,is that God's love is not dependent on you loving Him first. Wow! This should excite you. You don't need to perform to be loved. You are already loved.

We love Him because He first loved us.

- I John 4:19 (NKJV)

You are the Chosen of the Lord. You are God's first choice. You are so precious He tattooed you on the palm of His hands indelibly;

Behold, I have indelibly imprinted (tattooed a
picture of) you on the palm of each of My hands;

[O Zion] your walls are continually before Me.

Isaiah 49:16[AMPC]

So you are loved. Much more than you can ever imagine. You are the centre of His world. You are the apple of His eyes. If you don't receive any Valentine gifts, you are loved. God has given you the greatest gift of all - the gift of Jesus. It doesn't matter if you receive flowers or not, God created all the flowers in the world just for you. He's so committed to every little detail of your life. It never gets to a stage where God is no longer passionate about you, so if you're feeling sad or lonely, you can tell Him. He's ready, willing and able to help you. That's why He is called an ever present help in times of trouble. He will always be there for you.

... for He [God] Himself has said, I will not in any way fail you nor give you up nor leave you without support. [I will] not, [I will] not, [I will] not in any degree leave you helpless nor forsake nor let [you] down (relax My hold on you)! [Assuredly not!]

Hebrews 13:5[AMPC]

Another thing you need to note is that God wants you to be so full of His love before you go into a relationship and when you are full of God's love, the following happens:

1.   **You don't beg for love:** I was having a conversation with a young lady recently about her relationship and how things had gone south in the relationship. While we were talking she said, "I kept begging him but he wouldn't call me, chat with me, call me on my birthday, or remember me at all, what should I do?"

To be honest, I felt sad when I heard this question. It was a strong indication that she wasn't conscious of who she was and who loved her already. She had no idea how valuable she was, so she decided to sell herself cheap by begging another human being to love her. When you are full of God's love, whoever is entering your life is just an addition. They won't be the centre of your life. You can't build your happiness on the fickleness of human love when you are full of God's love.

If a man would give for love All the wealth of his house, It would be utterly despised.

- SOS 8:7 [NKJV]

2.   **All that comes out of you is Love:** By now you must have realized that you can't give out what you don't have. If you are not full of God's kind of love, you will struggle with loving anyone genuinely. Some people don't treat their partners kindly and this is because they are full of hate, bitterness and anger. When you're full of love even when your

partner is not behaving nice, all you have is love for them and that's all you will give them.

3.   You won't accept just anything. Empty people accept whatever comes their way. The Bible puts it this way; *A person who is full refuses honey, but even bitter food tastes sweet to the hungry.- Proverbs 27:7 [NLT]* . What this means is, when you're so desperate and empty, any kind of love is sweet. You won't mind being the tenth girlfriend because you'll be happy to accept the small crumbs of love falling to you. When you are full of God's love you won't want anyone treating you less than your Father, God, treats you. People are free to offer you what they like but you are also free to accept or decline their offer. This is why it annoys me when people reach out to me and say, "Pastor, this man beats me, cheats on me, uses me but he said he loves me, what should I do?" You can't be with a man that treats you without value and you're still even considering staying with him. It just shows that you are empty and desperate for love. If you are full of love, there are things you won't accept.

CHAPTER TWO

THE TRUTH ABOUT LOVE

If you want to know the truth about love you have to know God. God is love and love is God. There is no better way to learn about something than to learn from the person who created it. Unfortunately, God's design of love has been so corrupted and perverted by the devil, it is difficult to tell the difference. Love has been substituted for many things and this is why many relationships and marriages do not last anymore; the real foundation has been destroyed.

However, all hope is not lost. We can return to God's original plan for love. The true definition of love is in the Bible and if you consciously follow the guidelines and grow in the attributes of love as described in the Bible, you will never go wrong or make wrong choices.

1 Corinthians 13 is the perfect description of God's original plan for love.

Though I speak with the tongues of men and of angels, but have not love, I have become sounding brass or a clanging cymbal. ²And though I have the gift of prophecy, and understand all mysteries and all knowledge, and though I have all faith, so that I could remove mountains, but have not love, I am nothing. ³And though I bestow all my goods to feed the poor, and though I give my body to be burned, but have not love, it profits me nothing.

Love suffers long and is kind; love does not envy; love does not parade itself, is not puffed up; does not behave rudely, does not seek its own, is not provoked, thinks no evil; does not rejoice in iniquity, but rejoices in the truth; bears all things, believes all things, hopes all things, endures all things.

Love never fails. But whether there are prophecies, they will fail; whether there are tongues, they will cease; whether there is knowledge, it will vanish away. For we know in part and we prophesy in part. But when that which is perfect has come, then that which is in part will be done away.

When I was a child, I spoke as a child, I understood as a child, I thought as a child; but when I became a man, I put away childish things. For now we see in a mirror, dimly, but then face to face. Now I know in part, but then I shall know just as I also am known.

And now abide faith, hope, love, these three; but the greatest of these is love.

Anything outside this description of love is a lie. These are the parameters to look out for when looking for true love;

Love suffers long

Love is kind;

Love does not envy;

love does not parade itself,

Love is not puffed up;

Love does not behave rudely,

Love does not seek its own,

Love is not easily provoked,

Love thinks no evil

Love does not rejoice in iniquity, but rejoices in the truth;

Love bears all things, believes all things, hopes all things, endures all things.

Love never fails.

As a child of God, this is the life we have been called to live, a life of love. This is our model for love. It is possible to live like this with the help of the Holy Spirit of course. One way you can help yourself live in this reality is to confess this scripture to yourself everyday and meditate on it. Where the Bible says love, put your name there instead. For example;

Kingsley is long-suffering, Kingsley is Kind, Kingsley does not envy, Kingsley does not boast, Kingsley is not proud... If you can do this consistently, it will become your reality and you will be able to tell when love is true and when it is not.

CHAPTER THREE

BUILDING LOVE THAT LASTS

Once you are sure that your love is built on the right foundation, the next important step is to build on it. This is because love can grow and love can die depending on the investments you are making into it. Most people are in utter shock when the love in their relationship begins to wane. They felt it would last forever because it's genuine.

Love is like fire, as powerful and raging as fire is, it needs substance to burn. Once there is no substance to burn, fire no matter how great will die naturally. It's the same with the love relationship between you and your spouse. There has to be certain inputs to ensure it keeps burning. Here are two things you can do to keep the fire of love burning.

BE INTENTIONAL

Without intentionality, no matter how your love started, it will wane. This happens to a lot of couples. You need to understand that where you make investments is where you can reap dividends. If you are employed in an establishment, that is where you will earn your salary. In fact, in some organizations you are paid strictly on the work hours you invested. Your relationship or marriage is like that too. When you make deliberate investments in making your partner feel loved, the love in your relationship has no choice but to grow.

Usually, when my wife and I counsel couples who feel they married the wrong person because they don't feel that love connection anymore, we know what they need to work on most times is making a new love commitment to their spouses and this takes effort. It won't happen automatically. At the beginning of a relationship, most people are excited, they are high on emotional love, they make sacrifices, they do all the right things unconsciously. Spending quality time talking and being with one another was a priority, but as the relationship progressed they began to do less and less and as time went on, they began to do nothing at all. Things like calling one another became a huge task and making sacrifices became major points for disagreements because they had not learnt to move from emotional love to intentional love.

Emotional love involves doing all the right things to sustain your relationship but most times these actions are unconscious. Intentional love involves doing all the right things but this time you are conscious of why you are doing it. Good couples are compatible by chance, great couples are compatible by choice. So, if you want your love relationship to last, you need to make a decision to move from emotional love to intentional love.

BUILD FRIENDSHIP

When it comes to men and relationships, we can see from several studies conducted over the years that most men don't want to hang out with their lovers all day but they are more than happy to hang out with their friends all day. This is because most have no clue what to do with a lover but they know more than a thousand fun things to do with their friends.

In Titus 2:4, the elderly women were encouraged to train the younger women to love their husbands. If you look at it on the surface, you would think that scripture was referring to romantic love between couples but that's not it. Strong's Greek translation tells us specifically the kind of love couples are to build here and it calls it "Philos"; which is the friendship kind of love. So in essence, that scripture was saying, let the older women teach the younger women how to be friends with their husbands because that is the kind of love most men desire.

Women always find this confusing because at the beginning of a relationship the man is all over them, calling them, texting them and spending endless time with them but all of a sudden, he is always on his phone or laptop or hanging out with his friends and she feels left behind every single time.

As a woman, instead of getting upset and nagging, let it be a call to switch from being just his lover to being his friend.

Usually, when most men have issues at work or with their finances, it isn't uncommon to see them leave home and go to their friends for help or for comfort. The reason is obvious, they know the friendship zone is a no condemnation zone, it's a place where you can be vulnerable yet loved. It is a place where you can talk about everything; share your joys and mourn your defeats. It's a no drama, no nagging zone. And of course, good friends understand and value one another.

What this means for you as a woman is that you need to find out what he likes and start learning about it. If he likes football, it will be a good idea to learn about football and watch with him rather than nag him watching football every single time. You can also be creative about this. Get a couples football team T-shirt of his club for both of you. This way, he sees you as his friend because you are interested in the things that interest him.

A lot of women on the other hand have no clue what their husbands like. All they are interested in is how to clean the house and cook the meals. In such homes, even with large televisions screens, the man still leaves home to hang out with his friends in a tiny bar to watch their small screen. No matter how old a man becomes, he never outgrows friendships. And, being his friend is how you sustain love and remain vital in his life till death do you part. The truth is you might not be attracted sexually forever, but you can be friends forever.

Women also desire friendships. As a man, it's important you make her know that she comes before your male friends. Even though most men do not like being vulnerable, you, however, need to teach her and help her understand you better. Friendship gives women an outlet to share problems, thoughts, feelings, and triumphs with those they share a close bond with. Being friends with your wife gives her an emotional support system- offering a shoulder to cry on, lending a listening ear and boosting her confidence and self-esteem. So be genuinely interested in the things that matter to her; ask her about them and give your support without reservation. Hang out, go to fun places with her, spend time just having fun discussions with her while she is cooking, do the dishes with her, call her at work and find out about her day, just keep the conversation going, let her be the first person to know when anything happens to you, plan the details of your life together, and don't be the source of stress in her life.

Friendship is key. It keeps the bond of love between couples in place. Strive to build that friendship bond.

CONCLUSION

In order to really enjoy true love, you must first know the God who created love and who is love. If you do not know God you cannot experience or give anyone real love. Like the popular saying, you cannot give what you do not have.

God is the first person to ever show love and His kind of love is the original and purest form of love. How did He show us this love? He sent his only begotten son to die for us, even while we were yet sinners.

Romans 5:8(KJV) says, "But God commendeth his love toward us, in that, while we were yet sinners, Christ died for us."

John 3:16(KJV) says, "For God so loved the world, that he gave his only begotten Son, that whosoever believeth in him should not perish, but have everlasting life."

God loves you so much, He thought about you even before you were born; He knew you would need a Saviour so He sent his Son to die for you, long before you were born. He loves you regardless of what you have done or who you are. Nothing can ever change God's love for you; nothing can increase it and nothing can diminish it.

However, to experience God's love, you have to accept this love. You have to accept His Son into your life and acknowledge the sacrifice He made on the cross for you. You must confess your sins and accept Jesus into your heart.

If this is a decision you want to make today, please say this prayer;

Lord Jesus, come into my life; I accept you today as my Lord and Saviour. Forgive me my sin. Wash me with your blood. I receive the grace to serve you all the days of my life. Thank you, Father, for I am born again, in Jesus' mighty name. AMEN!

Welcome to God's family. Now that you have the purest form of love in your heart, you will begin to see it manifest in your life and in your relationships.

REFERENCES

Lisa Lombardi, (2023), Health Matters, An experts guide to your brain in love,

https://healthmatters.nyp.org/an-experts-guide - to - your - brain - in - love/#:~:text=Researchers%20have%20sc anned%20the%20brains,we're%20wild%20 about%20someone.

A.Pawlowski, (2017), How Long does Passion Last. Science says ..., TODAY, https://www.today.com/hea.th/how-long-does-passion-last-four-stages-love-t108471 Staci Lee Schnell, (2016), Scientific Advisory Board, https://psychcentral.com/blog/the- importance-off-friendship-in-marriage#1

Kelly Gonsalves, (2021), Is love at first sight real? Why it happens & 9 signs you're experiencingit,mbgrelationships,https://www.mi ndbodygreen.com/articles/love-at-first-sight

Florian Z., Matthias H., Cornelia W., Dick B., (2017), What kind of love is love at first sight?, Wiley Online Library, Personal Relationship, https://doi.org/10.1111/pere.12218

Loving More Than One Person At the Same

Time, (2021),
https://socialsci.libretexts.org/Bookshelves/Psych
ology/Book%3A_The_Meaning_of_Love_(Garlik
ov)/01%3A_Chapters/1.16%3A_Loving_More_T
han_One_Person_At_the_Same_Time

Zara Zareen, (2019), Is It Normal to Be Attracted
to Others While in a Relationship?, Medium,
https://medium.com/@zara.zareen/is-it-
normal-to-be-attracted-to-others-while-in-
a-relationship-
c6985d1edb4f#:~:text=In%20fact%2C%
20it's%20much%20more,in%20a%20long
%2Dterm%20relationship.

Dina Cheney, (2020), How To Handle A Crush
When You're Married (And What It Means),
m b g r e l a t i o n s h i p s ,
https://www.mindbodygreen.com/articles/deal-
with-crushes-when-married

Kelly Alexander, (2022), This is Why Female
Friendships are so Important, Escape Haven,
https://escapehaven.com/2022/07/female-
friendships/

OTHER BOOKS BY PASTORS MILDRED AND KINGSLEY OKONKWO

- 25 Wrong Reasons People Enter Into Relationships When Am I Ready?
- Just Us Girls
- 7 Things I Badly Want To Tell Women
- How To Know If He/She Really Loves You
- I Love You But My Parents Say No
- God Told Me To Marry You
- Should Ladies Propose?
- Waiting For Isaac
- 7 Questions Wise Women Ask
- 7 Qualities Wise Men Want
- A-z Of Marriage
- Chayil: Secrets Of The Virtuous Woman
- Praying For Your Husband
- Praying For Your Wife
- Help! My Husband Is Acting Funny
- All Year Round- For Men
- All Year Round- For Women
- Manual- The Way Men Think
- One Thing
- God Can Be Trusted - Volumes 1 & 2
- Heal Before You Deal
- No Dry Season: A devotional on financial prosperity for couples

Author's Profile

Kingsley Okonkwo is a Specialist when it comes to Relationships and Marriages. With over two decades hands-on experience as a Pastor, Relationship Coach, Counsellor and Author, PK, as he is fondly called is a presidential member of the American Association of Christian Counsellors, a board-certified Master Christian Life Coach and a certified Relationship Counsellor. He is renowned for Love and Relationships, Marriage and Family Life, Domestic Violence, Divorce and Infidelity Recovery.

He is the visionary behind the phenomenal Love, Dating and Marriage Ministry, widely known as LdmwithPK, a highly impactful relationship ministry with a reach of hundreds of thousands of people across the globe.

He has authored numerous books on relationships, a few of which he co-authored with his lovely wife and partner in ministry, Pastor Mildred and they are blessed with three adorable children.

To connect with the author ⟶

SCAN ME

Made in the USA
Columbia, SC
14 May 2025

57870688R00067